21-Days To A Better You
DAILY RENEWAL JOURNAL

DR. VANESSA HOWARD

HOWARD UNIVER-CITY, LLC

This book is a work of nonfiction. This journal

21-Days To A Better You: Daily Renewal Journal

Copyright © 2022 by Dr. Vanessa Howard
All rights reserved.

Without limiting the rights under copyright reserved above, no part of this publication may be reproduced, stored in, or introduced into a retrieval system, or transmitted, in any form, or by any means (electronic, mechanical, photocopying, recording, or otherwise) without the express written permission of both the copyright owner and the publisher of this book, except in the case of brief quotations embodied in critical articles and reviews. For permission, contact Dr. Vanessa Howard at www.drvanessahoward.com or www.howarducity.com

Email: drvhoward@gmail.com or vanessa@howarducity.com

The scanning, uploading, and distribution of this book via the Internet or via any other means without the permission of the owner is illegal and punishable by law. Please purchase only authorized electronic editions and do not participate in or encourage electronic piracy of copyrighted materials. Your support of the author's rights is appreciated.

Howard Univer-City, LLC

12685 Dorsett Road PMB 225

Maryland Heights, MO 63043-2380

TB ISBN: 978-1-7366987-6-1

Scripture quotations marked KJV are taken from the KING JAMES VERSION (KJV): KING JAMES VERSION, public domain.

PRINTED IN THE UNITED STATES OF AMERICA

ISBN 978-976-95586-7-0

❦ Created with Vellum

Renewing Your Mind

How Can 21-Days Help You Change a Habit?

Habits are behaviors that you repeat regularly, and it occurs subconsciously. In order to change a habit, you have to replace it with a new one. Committing to a goal for 21-straight days will help you establish change in your life. The goal for this journal is to help reboot and renew your mind so that you can live your best life. Using these affirmations, as it relates to the scriptures, is the beginning of your transformation. For 21 days, you will be resetting your thought processes to focus on the abundant life that God has prepared for you.

Why Do I Need To Say Positive Affirmations?

Positive comments are better — and more useful than negative ones. It takes FIVE positive comments to negate ONE negative comment that has been spoken over your life. There is life and death in the power of a person's word. Studies have found that regularly using positive affirmation rewires your brain.

Affirmations have the power to motivate you to act and think more positively. Affirmations is your faith talk to give you power to change negative thinking patterns and assist you in replacing them with positive thinking patterns. You can fundamentally change the structure of your mind within the next 21-days.

How to Use This Journal

For the next twenty-one days, you will start and finish your day with positive thoughts using the Word of God and positive affirmations.

Romans 12:2

Do not be conformed to this world, but be transformed by the renewal of your mind, that by testing you may discern what is the will of God, what is good and acceptable and perfect.

Write Your Vision

And the LORD answered me, and said, Write the vision, and make it plain upon tables, that he may run that readeth it. For the vision *is* yet for an appointed time, but at the end it shall speak, and not lie: though it tarry, wait for it; because it will surely come, it will not tarry.
Habakkuk 2:2-3

Song: "Write the Vision" Patrick Love & the A.L. Jinwright Mass

WHAT IS A VISION BOARD?

It's a visual representation of your goals, dreams or aspirations. Think carefully about what you want to displayed to remind you of what you want to accomplish.

Create a Vision Board to remind you of your goals. Include images, words that spark your motivation, things that remind you of your value, goals, or dreams. Include any kind of images and text to represent your vision. There is no right or wrong answer. Your goal is to craft something that will inspire you to realize your dreams and goals on a daily basis.

Use the next page to create your vision board.

My Vision

How to Use This Journal

FOR THE NEXT TWENTY-ONE DAYS, YOU WILL START AND FINISH YOUR DAY WITH POSITIVE THOUGHTS USING THE WORD OF GOD AND AFFIRMATIONS.

MORNING

- Read your daily affirmation and scripture, then pray and meditate on God's will for your life.
- Create a daily focus for yourself.

EVENING

- Write about one joyous thing that you experienced on that day. Focus on the good things that happened to you and for you.

Day 1: I Am An Amazing Gift

I am an amazing gift to myself and the world around me.

Psalms 139: 14

I will praise thee; for I am fearfully and wonderfully made; marvelous are thy works; and that my soul knoweth right well.

My goal for today is:

- _____
- _____

Evening Reflection: What brought you joy on today?

- _____
- _____
- _____
- _____

Day 2: I Am Loved

I love and appreciate myself. I appreciate my flaws and all because God is molding and making me

\

1 John 4:16
And we have known and believed the love that God hath to us. God is love; and he that dwelleth in love dwelleth in God, and God in him."

My goal for today is:

- _____
- _____

Evening Reflection: What brought you joy on today?

- _____
- _____
- _____
- _____

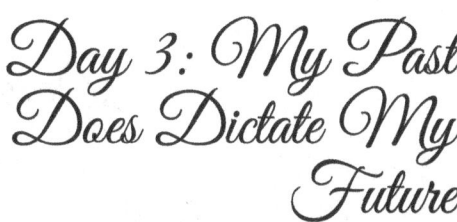

Day 3: My Past Does Dictate My Future

My past no longer matters. It has no control over me. What I do today will shape my future.

Philippians 3:13-14

¹³ Brethren, I count not myself to have apprehended: but this one thing I do, forgetting those things which are behind, and reaching forth unto those things which are before,

¹⁴ I press toward the mark for the prize of the high calling of God in Christ Jesus.

My goal for today is:

- _____
- _____

Evening Reflection: What brought you joy on today?

- _____
- _____
- _____
- _____

Day 4: My Peace is My Power

My peace is my power. I will rest and let God take care of all my problems.

Philippians 4:7
And the peace of God, which surpasses all understanding, will guard your hearts and your minds in Christ Jesus.

My goal for today is:

- _____
- _____

Evening Reflection: What brought you joy on today?

- _____
- _____
- _____
- _____

Day 5: God Is Sovereign

God is Sovereign over my life. Beyond what my eyes can see, God has a blessing in store for me.

Numbers 6:24-26

The Lord bless you and keep you; the Lord make his face to shine upon you and be gracious to you; the Lord lift up his countenance upon you and give you peace.

My goal for today is:

- _____
- _____

Evening Reflection: What brought you joy on today?

- _____
- _____
- _____
- _____

Day 6: I Am Thankful

I am thankful and grateful for the good in my life.

Luke 1:17

Every good gift and every perfect gift is from above, and cometh down from the Father of lights, with whom is no variableness, neither shadow of turning.

My goal for today is:

- _____
- _____

Evening Reflection: What brought you joy on today?

- _____
- _____
- _____
- _____

Day 7: Letting Go

I am letting go of all my worries and fears.

Philippians 4:19
But my God shall supply all of your needs according to his riches in glory by Christ Jesus

My goal for today is:

- _____
- _____

Evening Reflection: What brought you joy on today?

- _____
- _____
- _____
- _____

Day 8: My Steps Are Ordered

God will order my steps. He will satisfy my soul and give me the strength I need for today.

Isaiah 58:11

And the LORD shall guide thee continually, and satisfy thy soul in drought, and make fat thy bones: and thou shalt be like a watered garden, and like a spring of water, whose waters fail not.

My goal for today is:

- _____
- _____

Evening Reflection: What brought you joy on today?

- _____
- _____
- _____
- _____

Day 9: All Is Well

My body and soul will be healthy. All is well with me.

3 John 1:2
Beloved, I pray that all may go well with you and that you may be in good health, as it goes well with your soul.

My goal for today is:

- _____
- _____

Evening Reflection: What brought you joy on today?

- _____
- _____
- _____
- _____

Day 10: I Am Equipped

*I am equipped to handle my issues effectively. **God will bless me abundantly.***

2 Corinthian 9:8

And God is able to make all grace abound to you, so that having all sufficiency in all things at all times, you may abound in every good work.

My goal for today is:

- _____
- _____

Evening Reflection: What brought you joy on today?

- _____
- _____
- _____
- _____

Day 11: I Am Strong

I am stronger that I think. God will not let me fail.

Deuteronomy 31:6
Be strong and of a good courage, fear not, nor be afraid of them: for the LORD thy God, he *it is* that doth go with thee; he will not fail thee, nor forsake thee.

My goal for today is:

- _____
- _____

Evening Reflection: What brought you joy on today?

- _____
- _____
- _____
- _____

Day 12: I Will Be Okay

There are some things I can't change, and I'm OKAY with that.

Isaiah 41:10

Fear not, for I am with you; be not dismayed, for I am your God; I will strengthen you, I will help you, I will uphold you with my righteous right hand.

My goal for today is:

- _____
- _____

Evening Reflection: What brought you joy on today?

- _____
- _____
- _____
- _____

Day 13: Sing His Praises

I praise the Lord for goodness towards me. I will sing His praises to everyone I meet.

Psalm 27:6
And now shall mine head be lifted up above mine enemies round about me: therefore will I offer in his tabernacle sacrifices of joy; I will sing, yea, I will sing praises unto the LORD.

My goal for today is:

- _____
- _____

Evening Reflection: What brought you joy on today?

- _____
- _____
- _____
- _____

Day 14: God Love Me

God loves me. His mercy and grace will cover my transgressions.

Ephesian 2:4-5

4 But God, who is rich in mercy, for his great love wherewith he loved us, 5 Even when we are dead in sins, hath quickened us together with Christ, (by grace ye are saved)

My goal for today is:

- _____
- _____

Evening Reflection: What brought you joy on today?

- _____
- _____
- _____
- _____

Day 15: God Is Working

God is working on my behalf.

Philippians 2:13
For it is God who works in you, both to will and to work for his good pleasure.

My goal for today is:

- _____
- _____

Evening Reflection: What brought you joy on today?

- _____
- _____
- _____
- _____

I trust God's plan for my life. I am stronger than I think.
Jeremiah 29:11.

"'For I know the plans I have for you,' declares the Lord, 'plans to prosper you and not to harm you, plans to give you a hope and a future.'"

My goal for today is:

- _____
- _____

Evening Reflection: What brought you joy on today?

- _____
- _____
- _____
- _____

Day 17: I Have All That I Need

I have all that I need to get through this day.
Luke 12: 6-7

6 Are not five sparrows sold for two farthings, and not one of them is forgotten before God? 7 But even the very hairs of your head are all numbered. Fear not therefore: ye are of more value than many sparrows.

I will praise thee; for I am fearfully and wonderfully made; marvelous are thy works; and that my soul knoweth right well.

My goal for today is:

- _____
- _____

Evening Reflection: What brought you joy on today?

- _____
- _____
- _____
- _____

Day 18: God Is With Me

I will not fear because God is with me. He can handle anything that I face.

Joshua 1:9

"Have not I commanded thee? Be strong and of a good courage; be not afraid, neither be thou dismayed: for the LORD thy God *is* with thee whithersoever thou goest."

My goal for today is:

- _____
- _____

Evening Reflection: What brought you joy on today?

- _____
- _____
- _____
- _____

Day 19: Abundant Life

I deserve all that is good. God has made provisions for me.

John 10:10

The thief cometh not, but for to steal, and to kill, and to destroy I am come that they might have life, and that they might have it more abundantly.

My goal for today is:

- _____
- _____

Evening Reflection: What brought you joy on today?

- _____
- _____
- _____
- _____

Day 20: Joy and Peace

My day will be filled with joy and peace.

Psalm 27:6

Now the God of hope fill you with all joy and peace in believing, that ye may abound in hope, through the power of the Holy Ghost.

My goal for today is:

- _____
- _____

Evening Reflection: What brought you joy on today?

- _____
- _____
- _____
- _____

Day 21: Hope in Christ

My hope is in Christ.

Romans 5:1-4

1Therefore being justified by faith, we have peace with God through our Lord Jesus Christ: 2By whom also we have access by faith into this grace wherein we stand, and rejoice in hope of the glory of God. 3And not only *so*, but we glory in tribulations also: knowing that tribulation worketh patience; 4**And patience, experience; and experience, hope:** 5And hope maketh not ashamed; because the love of God is shed abroad in our hearts by the Holy Ghost which is given unto us.

My goal for today is:

- _____
- _____

Evening Reflection: What brought you joy on today?

- _____
- _____
- _____

22 Now What?

Develop A Lifestyle That Supports Changes

Hopefully this journal has help you to develop a renewed spirit of praise and thanksgiving. Remember that you replace an old habit with a new habit. Saying affirmations and studying the word will help you develop the behavioral patterns and self-control needed for an abundant life. Maintain your focus and preserver in your efforts to integrate praise into your daily life.

Change can be difficult because habits are deeply ingrained. Be patient with yourself for your change to occur.

Philippians 4:8

Finally, brethren, whatsoever things are true, whatsoever things are honest, whatsoever things are just, whatsoever things are pure, whatsoever things are lovely, whatsoever things are of good report; if there be any virtue, and if there be any praise, think on these things·

About the Author

Dr. Vanessa Howard, affectionately known as Dr. V, is an award-winning educator and author. Her motto is, "Discover Life, Literacy, and Legacy with Dr. V," all elements can be found in her body of work. Currently, she teaches at the university level and is a nation- wide speaker and literacy trainer.

Currently, I am collaborating with my granddaughter on a series of books entitled, "The Adventures of Nala." She struggled in the classroom using the writing process, so I provided support and tutoring at home. One day, as we edited one of her stories, we both spontaneously laughed. We shared the stories with our family and decided to have her best stories published.

In my free time, I enjoy spending quality time with my family and sewing.

I would love to connect with you on social media. Sociatap: https://bit.ly/DRV-Sociatap Website: http://www.howarducity.com

facebook.com/drvhoward

twitter.com/DrVanessaHowar1

instagram.com/drvhoward

Also By Dr. Vanessa Howard

REDEEMED: WITH GOD'S HELP WE CAN OVERCOME

I have an inspirational story being released March 2022 entitled, "Redeemed: With God's Help We Can Overcome." This book is in a standalone series "Grateful Hearts," written by national bestselling authors to encourage readers in a tangible way and provide experiences with scriptures as never before. My story explores Miriam, Moses' sister and I shared her life challenges and obstacles as they related to my life. You thought you knew Miriam before, but I will re-introduce you to this very complex woman. We will explore her flaws and understand that through God's redemptive power we can overcome any obstacles.

FROM THE PROJECTS TO A PH.D: A VIEW FROM THE OTHER SIDE OF AMERICA

#1 AMAZON BEST SELLING

Have you ever been kissed by a refreshing white cloud? Do you remember how its caress would leave you wanting more and waiting for its next lingering touch? White clouds were not strangers in the projects during the summer months. These refreshing vapors provided a welcome break from the sweltering heat of the sun's rays beating down on the concrete palaces that St. Louis called the projects. The fluffy mist was the unifying factor in the projects that all the kids loved. We inhaled the clouds and embraced the cooling mist as it danced around our bodies. Who would have thought that these mystical veils had the potential to destroy my hopes and dreams?

Dr. Vanessa Howard's book *From the Projects to a Ph.D.* discusses humble beginnings, challenges in pursuing higher education, and the determination needed to succeed. You will be inspired by the resiliency of the human spirit, as she shares personal insights, and experiences of racial inequities that shaped, but did not define her life.

Although her experiences shared in this book are not unique, they provide a glimpse into the "other side of America" rarely shared with other cultures. Within these pages, you will find strategies to assist readers in becoming more culturally responsive. She prays this story will be a catalyst for change and offer hope to those who need it most. When we know better, we should do better. This is a must-read for those who are passionate about reform in the areas of education, law, gender equity, and racial justice.

www.ingramcontent.com/pod-product-compliance
Lightning Source LLC
Chambersburg PA
CBHW011959090526
44590CB00023B/3790